The Inspired Entrepreneur

*366 Days of Inspiration for
the Entrepreneur*

Heather Hope Reed

Aligned Publishing

This book is dedicated to my Wonderful Husband, Roger, and the amazing Gizmo, my Yorkie.

Contents

Introduction

This book is for you, the entrepreneur! Use it daily to help you to move forward in your business and your life. Each day is a gentle reminder of the law of attraction and how it helps with your business.

When you feel an impulse to flip to a random page, it is the Universe sending you a message you need to hear.

To have an even further discussion, go to my podcast for the day you are reading. I expand on each day. https://anchor.fm/theinspiredentrepreneur

Have fun with it.
Life is supposed to be fun.

Yours truly,

Heather Hope Reed

Preface

Being an Entrepreneur can be very challenging at times, especially if you are working at home. These past several months have been most challenging as the World found itself told to stay home.

Right before everything came about, I had a vision to write a book. I was standing in the shower of my manifested ocean view home and an entire download came over me. I started writing that book right away! This isn't the same book, but the vision of my life is still here as I finish this one.

Many months passed, with the same desire to write a book but the one from earlier didn't feel exciting anymore. I know not to keep pushing against something that no longer feels interesting or appealing. So, I let it go for a bit. I let go of the "trying to figure it out" part of my mind knowing that the answer will come.

One day, while driving around town, a series of thoughts came through my mind. I remember in one Abraham Hicks' recording that a woman was asking about Esther's next book. "When was it coming out?" She asked. Abraham told her that Esther comes on stage every Saturday and delivers an entire book to us and we should appreciate that.

I thought about the meaning of what they said. I also knew I didn't want to write an entire book because writing books is a lot of writing (this is my 9th book). Something came over me in that moment and I realized that all my writing on my Facebook page was a book! I had written daily for 2 years on my topic. Surely that's a book!

One thing led to the next and I was inspired to write a daily inspiration book for Entrepreneurs. The Inspired Entrepreneur was born! The book was ALREADY written. All I had to do is pull it off the internet and into a book format.

I'm not one who likes to recreate the wheel. That makes things feel hard to do.

At the very same time, I also realized the topic of my podcast I wanted to start. Each day in my book will be short and sweet while my podcast will be the longer version of each day. So, I created a DAILY podcast based off of this very book! I started it a week later, September 1, 2020. I can talk a lot. I can talk for hours about the law of attraction. A daily podcast is perfect! At least for the first year. (You can find it here: https://anchor.fm/theinspiredentrepreneur)

What you're doing doesn't have to be complicated. I learned this lesson to LET IT BE EASY!

While putting this book together I have had moments that I felt a bit moody. I would read through a few days worth and it instantly was what I needed to read! Each time I walked away thinking that this book is truly wonderful.

When you receive this book, place it on your desk as a daily reference. Flip to the day, read it, take it in, maybe check out the podcast, feel inspired. Each day will remind you of something you may need to hear.

Other times, when you feel like you need extra inspiration, pick up the book, flip to a page, read, read a few more if you like, feel inspired. Receive the message.

January 1

T o allow a lot more money in you need to let go of the limiting beliefs about money.

The Inspired Entrepreneur

January 2

If you can relax about when your manifestations will
occur, they will come to you faster.

Heather Hope Reed

January 3

To attract more prosperity into your life:

1. Feel the feelings of EASE, FREEDOM, SECURITY, ABUNDANCE more often than not.

2. Be happy most, if not all of the time.

3. Follow inspiration. Understand you are an extension of source energy and being guided all the time.

The Inspired Entrepreneur

January 4

If your ideas are from source there's no need for validation from others.

It's already validated!

Heather Hope Reed

January 5

I t just takes focus on what you want to become a Vibrational Match.

The Inspired Entrepreneur

January 6

You always have to follow the strong impulses you have.

Heather Hope Reed

January 7

The more I talk about how I want to see my business go the more my business goes that way.

It's just really cool to see it in action.

Every time I talk about someone signing up to work with me, they sign up to work with me.

It happens easily when I'm talking about it without resistance. It's just a passing thought. ❤

Be free about it.

The Inspired Entrepreneur

January 8

The only way to get beyond your current reality is to look beyond your current reality.

Heather Hope Reed

January 9

F ocus on the future that you want.

When you focus on your current reality that becomes your future.

January 10

More of the same is not what you came here for. You came for more.

Expansion!

Heather Hope Reed

January 11

The universe said yes.
All you have to do is line up with it.
Know it's done. Get ready for it. Act as if it's already in physical form.

I want you to KEEP moving forward.
Keep focused on what you want, not what you don't want.

January 12

As you allow yourself to dream, you are creating a new reality.

Heather Hope Reed

January 13

S top looking for clients and start looking for the vibration of a successful business.

The Inspired Entrepreneur

January 14

T oday, something really hit me to think MUCH BIGGER.

Looking at the big brains of our past and present, we are all capable of creating ANYTHING.

If you're going to dream and visualize, GO BIG!

Heather Hope Reed

January 15

You ask by the attention to give to it.

You get what you focus on whether you want it or not.

The Inspired Entrepreneur

January 16

Are you expecting success or failure? You get whatever you expect.

Heather Hope Reed

January 17

S trategy does not sell.
It's your vibration that sells.
It's your beliefs that sell.

It's your mindset that sells.

The Inspired Entrepreneur

January 18

Two mornings in a row I woke up to the question, "are you stepping into all that you are?"

My thoughts continue in my mind as I'm half asleep.

"You are so powerful. Go all in. Step into everything you want. Everything you are."

It's time. It's time for you to step into everything. It's time for you to be that powerful creator. It's time to step up and be all you are. All that is inside of you.

Heather Hope Reed

January 19

T he secret is to focus on where you're going rather than where you've been or where you are.

Tip the scales of where your focus is directed.

The Inspired Entrepreneur

January 20

T he one with the strongest vibration wins.
Don't wobble.

Heather Hope Reed

January 21

Whatever is active in your vibration is what's manifesting.

Pay attention to what you're focusing on. It's really that easy.

January 22

"**R**eally, there are no absolute Right and absolute Wrong choices. Just make one and line up with it. Better, line up with it and then make it. But if you've already made it, then line up with it."

"There's no right or wrong in anything. There's just You in relation to what you've Become...to what you're Allowing yourself to Experience." -Abraham Hicks

I love knowing this!

You are so powerful that you make anything work. Just line up with it.

Heather Hope Reed

January 23

If you're feeling confused on what to do next, it's vital you relax for a bit until you receive your next impulse to act.

Just relax.

The Inspired Entrepreneur

January 24

F ollow the fun.
If it's not fun, stop and do something fun.

Heather Hope Reed

January 25

O nly choose what you really desire.
Then it comes right in.

The Inspired Entrepreneur

January 26

There's more available to you.

Heather Hope Reed

January 27

"Talk as if what you want is in the process of coming." -Abraham Hicks

The Inspired Entrepreneur

January 28

F ocus on the whole vision of the life you want. Focus on it, feel it every single day.

You will become a vibrational match to it and it will appear.

Heather Hope Reed

January 29

There is no time frame for anything. Get into the vibration of it and follow impulses.

The Inspired Entrepreneur

January 30

R ight now is a brand new moment.

Heather Hope Reed

January 31

Y ou vibrate at the level you want to be and you will immediately attract steps to it.

I'm not even kidding. Immediate results.

The Inspired Entrepreneur

February 1

T he life you keep living is the life you are a vibrational match to.

If you want to change your life you must change it vibrationally first.

That's the key to having more in your life.

Heather Hope Reed

February 2

My goals every single day are:
To feel good, really really good.
To be happy.
To make sure I have fun.
When these are happening, I make more money with total ease.

I have lots to share. Lots to give.

My attraction magnet is full on. So no matter where I am good things are coming into my existence automatically.
Make sure you are feeling really good. That's all that matters.

The Inspired Entrepreneur

February 3

The amount of daydreaming, visualizing, and scenarios I've done makes this feel normal.

Next logical step.

Heather Hope Reed

February 4

How often do you visualize your rich life?

Your Millionaire life.

Your imagination is your best friend.

Focus your mind on the feeling of abundance and prosperity.

Visualize the life you intend to live. Do this daily. Tip the scales of what you're focusing on.

When you tip the scales, manifestation happens so quickly!

Become a vibrational match to your desires.

The Inspired Entrepreneur

February 5

Visualize your millionaire life as much as you can.

Write your perfect Millionaire life each day.

Tip the scales of where you put your attention.

This is it!!

Heather Hope Reed

February 6

Watch it!
What you focus on is what you're asking for more.

It's not about the words you use so much as what you have your attention on.

The Inspired Entrepreneur

February 7

Affirmations work.

They are just new thoughts that will call in what you want.

Your words are powerful!

Heather Hope Reed

February 8

E ach morning, write in your journal a perfect day in the life you are aspiring to live - your dream life.

You are writing your future into existence.

Your future is now. At ANY moment you can manifest what you want.

The Inspired Entrepreneur

February 9

You gotta stop trying so hard.
Let it flow with ease.

Heather Hope Reed

February 10

C ompletely let go and trust.
Go with the flow.
Get everything you want.

The Inspired Entrepreneur

February 11

Visualize it, daydream about it, write about it, think about it a lot, get excited about it, daily.

Heather Hope Reed

February 12

" **C** hoose a thought, pretend that it's already happened. be excited about it, watch what happens." -Abraham Hicks

The Inspired Entrepreneur

February 13

The more you listen to your inner guidance the faster your desires manifest.

You are being led to everything you want, are you paying attention?

Are you believing?

Are you taking time for yourself to enjoy life?

It's easier to hear when you're enjoying life.

Heather Hope Reed

February 14

D o what you love and the money will follow.

It follows because you're passionate, you're in alignment living happily ever after.

The Inspired Entrepreneur

February 15

Get into the vibration of what you want by only focusing on what it is you want and why do you want it.

Look at pictures, daydream about it, be happy about it. But don't ask how it's going to happen and don't feel discouraged.

Get happy and excited about its existence. See yourself there.

Heather Hope Reed

February 16

E xpect success because the universe has it lined up.

The Inspired Entrepreneur

February 17

Stay focused on your dreams, as that's how they become a reality.

Heather Hope Reed

February 18

W rite in your journal or notebook:
"The things that are DONE:"

List out all the things that you want to have.
Write, DONE, next to each.

Start thinking and believing they are done.

It's done, it's done, it's DONE.

Now, live from that space of KNOWING it's all done.

Then, live happily ever after.

The Inspired Entrepreneur

February 19

Alignment makes it easy. If it's not easy you're not in alignment.

Stop and feel yourself back into an ease state then go from there.

This is important. The feeling of alignment with your inner being is excitement, happiness, bliss, fun, ease.

The feeling of fear is not in alignment and will bring more effort and work for you.

Alignment is ease. Ease feels so good!

Heather Hope Reed

February 20

Get excited about the money that is about to break through to you!

Stop looking at lack and start looking at what is about to happen.

Get excited. Feel good.

Start spending it vibrationally.

Have fun!

The Inspired Entrepreneur

February 21

Practice being happy.

Notice moments that give you joy.

Relish in that feeling.

Get happy!

Get happy and then everything wonderful will be attracted to you.

Heather Hope Reed

February 22

Only do what feels good.

If you feel fear, you are out of alignment.

Get back into alignment first!

Then take the inspired action.

The Inspired Entrepreneur

February 23

Set your vibration in the morning and watch your day go according to it.

Heather Hope Reed

February 24

"Do everything you can think of to put you in the place of expecting the outcome that you want. Just do everything you can think of. There is not a downside to that." -Abraham Hicks

The Inspired Entrepreneur

February 25

"**W**hen you're having trouble making a decision, you're making it too soon."
-Abraham Hicks

Line up the energy of what you want to have.

Once the energy is lined up it becomes easier.

Allow inspiration to guide you.

Heather Hope Reed

February 26

You create through your focus.

That's how everything is created.

If you want a successful business, focus on having a successful business.

Period.

The end.

The Inspired Entrepreneur

February 27

Be light about everything.

When you are light, easy, you have a lot less resistance about it.

That's key.

Heather Hope Reed

February 28

"**P**rocrastination is the wisdom to not force anything you're not vibrationally ready for."
-Abraham Hicks

February 29

E very morning I answer the question: Who am I?
The identity I have created and keep expanding
on is what I answer.

I start my day as that person.

Who are you?

Heather Hope Reed

March 1

Q uick Tip:

Every time you think positive thoughts about your business you become a magnet to attract new clients.

It is THAT easy.

March 2

Watch the things that you say because you are attracting those very things to you.

Just because it happens to others does NOT mean it has to happen to you!

You believing that it's 'how it is' is what makes it that way in your life.

Change it to something that you DO want.

Heather Hope Reed

March 3

The easier you are with sales, the easier the sales will be.

The Inspired Entrepreneur

March 4

S ay it with me:

"I am attracting dream clients who love to pay me."

Heather Hope Reed

March 5

If you realized how powerful your thoughts are, you'd never think another negative thought again.

The Inspired Entrepreneur

March 6

"When you follow your bliss you are always on your path." -Abraham Hicks

Heather Hope Reed

March 7

Y our job is to get ready for what the universe has ready for you.

The Inspired Entrepreneur

March 8

"It's not luck, it's alignment. You're not lucky, you're aligned." -Abraham Hicks

Heather Hope Reed

March 9

Your successful business is already done - you just have to line up with it.

The Inspired Entrepreneur

March 10

You can have anything you want - you just have to focus on it.

Heather Hope Reed

March 11

There's always another way. (There are probably a million other ways.)

The Inspired Entrepreneur

March 12

Take time to daydream, fantasize, relax, and think about what you want to create.

Heather Hope Reed

March 13

" **T**he more expansive your thoughts are the more expansive the reality you create."
-Sanaya Roman

The Inspired Entrepreneur

March 14

Believe in your success!
Picture yourself having what you want.

Heather Hope Reed

March 15

"**U**nlimited thinking puts you in touch with the larger vision picture of your life and links you with vision of your higher self."
-Sanaya Roman

You have the ability to generate new ideas that will take you to the higher levels in your life and work by attracting them.

The Inspired Entrepreneur

March 16

C heck in with what you're doing periodically to see if you're feeling good.

Ask:

Am I having a good time?

Do I feel good?

Am I having fun?

Heather Hope Reed

March 17

G oing with the flow means you have to stop trying to figure it out.

When you try to figure it out you put resistance on your path.

Just let it go.

Focus on feeling good and watch the path unfold.

The Inspired Entrepreneur

March 18

B ecome a believer of the vibrational version for it to become a physical version.

Heather Hope Reed

March 19

Make a list of the things you want to make physical, put it some place you'll see it daily, talk about those topics.

Keep talking about the things coming!
Talk about them until they pop into existence.
You get to decide what you make true in your life.

But, here's the kicker: you gotta talk about these things in a positive way.
Line up with it
Watch how much "efforting" you're doing and relax it a bit.
Then, relax it even more. Then, go take a nap.

The Inspired Entrepreneur

March 20

E njoy the journey because it's the longest part.

Heather Hope Reed

March 21

I t's not about "feeling the fear and doing it anyway;" it's about "feeling the alignment and then being excited about doing it!"

This is important. The feeling of alignment with your inner being is excitement, happiness, bliss, fun, ease.

The feeling of fear is not in alignment and will bring more effort and work for you.

Alignment is ease. Ease feels so good!

The Inspired Entrepreneur

March 22

In business, you must follow what feels good to you. If you keep following what others tell you, you'll be all over the place.

What feels good to you is what works best.

Heather Hope Reed

March 23

If your business is not growing on autopilot, (and I don't mean Facebook ads), you need to adjust your vibration.

When you're in alignment and have your energy on fire, it will grow rapidly, with ease.

The Inspired Entrepreneur

March 24

T here never has to be a "sales conversation." Or, "trying to close a client."

When you decide what you want, the universe LINES IT UP. LINES UP THE PERFECT CLIENTS FOR YOU. You never ever ever ever have to ever convince ANYONE to work with you.

The way it works is that everyone just KNEW they wanted to work with me. IT'S A KNOWING.

We are connected energetically.

I've never made a rule to have sales calls, so I never had to do them.

Everything else COMPLICATES it all. All the sales stuff you are learning out there is completely complicating allowing things to be EASY for you.

Heather Hope Reed

March 25

You get to set the rules in your business.

The Inspired Entrepreneur

March 26

Quick Tip:

Every time you think positive thoughts about your business you become a magnet to attract new clients.

It is THAT easy.

Heather Hope Reed

March 27

When your energy is powerful regarding your business, people will be COMPELLED to click on your link. Or, on your Facebook page.

They won't know why they need to take a look but they won't have any control over it.

That's how powerful you can be.

That's how powerful energy is.

March 28

E verything Is supposed to be easy.
Alignment makes it easy.

Heather Hope Reed

March 29

Alignment brings the money.
It brings it easily.

The Inspired Entrepreneur

March 30

Alignment makes it easy. If it's not easy you're not in alignment.

Stop and feel yourself back into an ease state then go from there.

Heather Hope Reed

March 31

You must keep your eye on what you want to see instead of what is.

Each morning, think about the things you want.

Envision them.

Smile and know they are happening.

Before you fall asleep, do that again.

Soon, things will begin to happen.

The Inspired Entrepreneur

April 1

Take the action when you are really feeling inspired to do so.

If you're just trying to make things happen it will fall short of what you're wanting.

Often nothing ever moves when you're trying to make it happen. Then, you get frustrated and say nothing ever works.

Get into alignment, get in a good mood, feel good, then follow the ideas that will flow.

Heather Hope Reed

April 2

Vibrational alignment with your desire. Stop putting timelines on things. Just line up to your desire.

The Inspired Entrepreneur

April 3

If it feels hard, it means you're not working from alignment.

It feels exciting and energetic when you work from alignment.

It's delicious.

Heather Hope Reed

April 4

I sn't your happiness the most important?

When you're happy your point of attraction is in alignment with the things you want.

See how it goes, follow your bliss and money will follow (not just from your job!).

April 5

As soon as my energy is aligned with my desires I'll be jumping up and out the door to live more life!

You have to get your energy going.
You have to get into Alignment.
You have to calibrate to source.
Then it becomes easy.

Heather Hope Reed

April 6

The only work there is: the work of staying in alignment.

The rest is easy.

The Inspired Entrepreneur

April 7

I t's not "a numbers game," it's an alignment game. Period.

Heather Hope Reed

April 8

Did you know that vibrational alignment is what makes people flock to you?

You are literally a magnet.

This is how the law of attraction can transform your business!

If you spent a lot more time on your vibration, you'd have a lot more sales.

The Inspired Entrepreneur

April 9

Only do what feels good.
If you feel fear, you are out of alignment.
Get back into alignment first!

Then take the inspired action.

Heather Hope Reed

April 10

Do you ever have those moments of complete utter frustration about not manifesting money?

I've had those moments. Many of them. Then I learned how to get past those moments of almost depression and hopelessness to allow money to come in.

It takes stable, ongoing alignment.

Being able to control my alignment has helped me on the path to increasing money to come in from many places.

Get yourself in a better mood as quickly as you can. With each positive thought will bring another positive thought and another. That's the law of attraction with your thoughts. You have to get yourself in a good mood to attract money (and clients) easily.

April 11

Stop asking where the money is...
When you are consistently in alignment you won't be asking, you'll be happy without it.

Then, everything comes in easily.

That's how it works.

Heather Hope Reed

April 12

There is no competition when you're in alignment.

It's your reality, there's only competition when you think there is..

Start claiming that you're the best and only option.

The Inspired Entrepreneur

April 13

L istening to your impulses...

Within the law of attraction, it's been said a million times that action needs to be a part of the manifestation.

That is correct. But, only inspired action.

How do you go about inspired action? You listen to your impulses.

But, Heather, I don't hear anything. (This is a common thing).

Do you know that intuition that you have... that's what we are talking about. That is your inner guidance that is guiding you all day, every day.

It's soft and gentle guiding. When you just know what to do next.

April 14

When you're in alignment, AKA, feeling good, your thoughts are in line with Source (your inner being), that means the thoughts that run through your mind are good.

They are on point.

The Inspired Entrepreneur

April 15

A KEY piece of manifesting exactly what you want is taking Inspired Action.

The Key to inspired action is actually taking action when you feel that nudge to take action.

The way I run my entire business is strictly through this key.

When you know what you want, the action will be natural. Or you may not have to take any action at all. It can just come to you.

Heather Hope Reed

April 16

T he most important thing to focus on is FEELING GOOD.

Get on your high flying disc and allow the universe to transform time and space for you.

The Inspired Entrepreneur

April 17

When you manage your Alignment consistently, you will be able to decide what you want and how to live, with confidence that the universe lines it all up.

The money shows up.

The opportunity shows up.

Everything works out for you.

Get yourself happy, trust, know, allow.

Heather Hope Reed

April 18

Vibrational Marketing is about getting yourself into vibrational alignment with your dream clients.

Lining up the energy. You become a magnet that attracts your clients who want what you are offering.

You are literally a MAGNET of energy. You are either attracting or repelling people.

You don't even need to speak to people to get them to find you. They just find you.

You get into alignment and you follow impulses.

That's the EASIEST way to live and work a business.

The easiest way to make money.

The easiest way to do EVERYTHING.

Line up the energy and follow your thoughts.

April 19

R emember, you wobble, they wobble.
If you start to worry, things start to wobble.
If you start to feel anxious, things start to wobble.

If you second guess, things start to wobble.

If you have confidence, things are stable.
If you feel relaxed, things are good.
If you are in alignment, everything is working out.
The more you chill, the easier it all becomes.

Heather Hope Reed

April 20

Did you know YOU get to create rules for your business? Would you like to see some of mine? (Creating rules means that's just how it is.)

My rules:

I always make good decisions.

When I'm in alignment, all is well.

I get paid daily. I don't message anyone to get clients, Clients just find me and instantly know they want to work with me. My clients sign up without sales calls. My clients know they can reach out when they need me. I know without a doubt my clients will have massive results. I only do what I feel like doing.All is well. Everything I do is enough. This is exactly how my business runs. With ease.

Has this inspired you to create rules for yours?

April 21

Ask for even more than you have asked for already, expand what is possible.

Heather Hope Reed

April 22

I magine that you already have what you want. How is your life different?

Next spend your vision to include those things.

April 23

Start your day with uplifting thoughts.

"Yes I can do this!" "Today is going to be amazing!"

Say these as soon as you open your eyes in the morning.

Heather Hope Reed

April 24

Set your intention before you start your day or project.

What is it that you want to have happen?

The Inspired Entrepreneur

April 25

Focus on the one thing in your business that excites you - even if it doesn't make sense.

Heather Hope Reed

April 26

Get clear on what you desire the most, make sure your desires don't contradict each other.

The Inspired Entrepreneur

April 27

If you're not motivated or inspired to do something don't do it until you are, if you can.

Heather Hope Reed

April 28

D o the thing that excites you first, don't put it off. That is your guidance directing you on your path.

The Inspired Entrepreneur

April 29

T ake "fun breaks" as soon as you feel bogged down.

Heather Hope Reed

April 30

Make sure you're having fun on the journey because the journey is longer than the destination.

May 1

D o you really want what you think you want?

Take a look at the essence of what you want to see if it lines up with what you want.

Heather Hope Reed

May 2

K now exactly what you want, focus on why, never on the how.

May 3

Be happy for the success of others.

They are showing you what you can have as well.

Heather Hope Reed

May 4

T urn off the TV, pay attention to what you put you are paying attention to.

The Inspired Entrepreneur

May 5

There's no competition, what you want is yours, there's more than enough for everyone.

Heather Hope Reed

May 6

You can only have what you believe you can have.

The Inspired Entrepreneur

May 7

If you can have the thought, you can have the thing.

Heather Hope Reed

May 8

Pay attention to where your time goes, is it positive uplifting activities?

May 9

Think good, loving thoughts about your clients.

Heather Hope Reed

May 10

Who are the influencers in your life? Are they uplifting or full of drama? Fear?

Remember, everyone you put your focus on has the ability to influence you.

The Inspired Entrepreneur

May 11

D o the work you are passionate about.
Don't do it for the money, do it for the fun you
get from it.

Heather Hope Reed

May 12

G et into alignment first, then start your work
day.

The Inspired Entrepreneur

May 13

Imagine the success of your clients and others around you.

Heather Hope Reed

May 14

Take exceptional care of yourself.

The better you care about yourself the better others will benefit and take care of you too.

The Inspired Entrepreneur

May 15

How you feel about your business is how others will perceive it.

Heather Hope Reed

May 16

Feel good about every single purchase you make.

The Inspired Entrepreneur

May 17

W hen you get an idea, don't over-analyze it. Just follow it a bit and see where it takes you.

You just never know where it may lead until you follow.

Heather Hope Reed

May 18

Y our path – the path to what you want is the path that feels the best.
That's how you know the path.

The Inspired Entrepreneur

May 19

C reating affirmations:

When ctreating them, decide on what it is that you want as what you say will become your reality.

What affirmations can you create today that will give you what you want in your business?

Heather Hope Reed

May 20

Y ou are powerful!

You have the same energy that creates worlds. Remember that.

You can have anything you desire. You just have to claim it with your words and thoughts.

The Inspired Entrepreneur

May 21

C lose your eyes, breathe, relax, keep breathing, feel any tension fade away.

Repeat as often as needed.

This is what it feels like to release resistance.

Heather Hope Reed

May 22

You are being guided. Relax and follow the thoughts that come in.

That is your Divine guidance gently directing you to everything you want.

May 23

Allow the universe to be your marketing department.

Follow what feels fun to you and trust your clients will be on the path of most fun.

Heather Hope Reed

May 24

Unlimited abundance is all around you.

Go outside and appreciate the natural abundance.

The more you appreciate what already is, the more you will have to appreciate.

The Inspired Entrepreneur

May 25

T he more you focus on something - the more you naturally draw it to you.

The most important question is: what are you focusing on?

Heather Hope Reed

May 26

When you are doing work you love - you become more magnetic to money.

In fact, you become magnetic to everything you want.

May 27

D oing work you love will change as you expand. Pay attention to what you are loving, it may surprise you.

Heather Hope Reed

May 28

L et go of trying to figure out how much money will be made by doing certain work.

When you follow the inspiration the money will be much more than you can figure.

The Inspired Entrepreneur

May 29

Look back at how successful you've already been in your life, and you will attract even more success.

Heather Hope Reed

May 30

Decide what you want and talk yourself into it. That's all.

The Inspired Entrepreneur

May 31

I f you don't want something to happen, don't think about it. Ever.

If you do, quickly change to a totally different thought.

Heather Hope Reed

June 1

F eel it - feel how it feels to have it if you can tap into the feeling of having it before you have it, it will manifest. It's vibrational.

You have to match the vibration of what you want in order to have it.

The Inspired Entrepreneur

June 2

L et go of the outcome.

Follow what feels good and exciting.

Allow the universe to give you everything you want.

Heather Hope Reed

June 3

All you have to do is line up to your dream.

Line up your thoughts to what you are wanting.

The Inspired Entrepreneur

June 4

Keep expanding your vision!

Heather Hope Reed

June 5

I f you wake up with thoughts of what to do next in your business (or anything) get up and do it.

First thing in the morning is a great time to receive inspiration from source.

Don't doubt or put it off. Follow the inspiration.

June 6

"**Y**ou're not manifesting, you're creating the environment that allows the manifestation."
-Abraham Hicks

Heather Hope Reed

June 7

F ind any excuse to feel good.
Then the law of attraction will add to it.

The Inspired Entrepreneur

June 8

T alk like a millionaire to become a millionaire.

Heather Hope Reed

June 9

C reate the content you love to create.

Use the platforms you love to use.

The guru is YOU. You know best.

Tap into your brilliance.

June 10

I f something feels interesting to you, follow that.
Just follow what is interesting to you.
You're being guided.

Heather Hope Reed

June 11

Repeat after me: I appreciate the abundance in my life.

June 12

Question for you: How often are you practicing good feeling thoughts?

Heather Hope Reed

June 13

L ine up the thoughts to what you want.
That creates the momentum.

Momentum is what gets you moving.

You getting moving is what brings joy.

And, the things you want.

June 14

Y ou want bigger results than you've been getting?

Stop jumping in too soon.

Allow the momentum to BUILD up before taking action.

OK, think about it.

It's the same for everything.

Take action when you CANNOT NOT take action.

That's the key to more explosive results.

Heather Hope Reed

June 15

M anifestations often come along and you don't even realize it.

Then, one day you look around and discover that things you wanted are already here!

It came so naturally. So organically. So much so that you didn't even know it.

Wow. That's living in the moment.

The Inspired Entrepreneur

June 16

W hen you are doing the things that you LOVE to do, you are in the ZONE.

If you're not feeling that massive buzz of energy, you may not be doing things you love.

That energy is CREATION happening!

That's what is moving you toward everything you want.

Heather Hope Reed

June 17

You're not trying to get clients, you are attracting them.

It's much easier to attract than it is to try to get.

Trying requires effort, attracting requires ease.

I like ease.

The Inspired Entrepreneur

June 18

Your thoughts are the important things. The power is in the thought you think.

Heather Hope Reed

June 19

W hen you wake in the morning...

Before getting up, lie there all snuggled in your sheets and pillows...

Smile and think about how amazing it is to start a brand new day.

That today will be an extraordinary day!

Something wonderful will happen today.

Then, jump out of bed excited to see what will happen!

The Inspired Entrepreneur

June 20

T onight, before you go to bed, think about how you'd like to see your day go tomorrow.

What wonderful things would you like to happen?

As soon as you close your eyes, think about the amazing sleep you're about to have. And, how you will wake up at your favorite time, refreshed and ready to have a great day!

If you do the pre-paving, you will, as soon as tonight, see results.

It's all about your intention.

Heather Hope Reed

June 21

Don't take score too soon.

When you check to see if something is working you may introduce resistance if what you're seeing is not what you had hoped for.

Keep doing the things that you truly enjoy and when you keep doing them everything will fall into place (and in a greater way than you could imagine!)

The Inspired Entrepreneur

June 22

The ease of things coming to you comes from you creating the vibrational environment for the attraction.

You are a magnet. You attract what you put out with how you feel.

Make how you feel the most important thing in your life because everything else falls into place perfectly.

Heather Hope Reed

June 23

Always follow your passions!

The energy that comes from following your passion is like NOTHING else.

That energy is PRICELESS.

It's the same energy that creates worlds.

The Inspired Entrepreneur

June 24

To have a lot more results in life you have to first make a decision on what it is that you want.

Then, secondly, you have to line up with that decision.

Heather Hope Reed

June 25

How do you pick one thing right now? (This is only if you really do need to make up your mind about what to do next.)

One way is to pick one, line up with it, and see how you feel.

If it feels really good then you're on the right path. If you don't feel good about that choice, then you know and you can choose again.

But, when you waver back and forth between two things it can get difficult to get anything because your energy is not fully lining up.

Make a decision, line up with it, see how you feel.

June 26

"Let your imagination be a bigger part of your experience and your observation be a lesser part of your experience." -Abraham Hicks

Heather Hope Reed

June 27

"When you stop needing it to make sense, then you'll make dollars." -Bashar

The Inspired Entrepreneur

June 28

You have to believe in the unbelievable.

Heather Hope Reed

June 29

Your strong determination with what you desire will make it so.

The Inspired Entrepreneur

June 30

Make sure the people around you are of the influence you want.

We are all influencers in this world.

Do they have the money mindset you desire?

Are they driven?

Do they have a powerful positive mindset?

Heather Hope Reed

July 1

When you take the importance out of the things you want they can make their way to you a lot more quickly.

The Inspired Entrepreneur

July 2

Today, I will feel good.

I will follow what feels good to me.

I know that if I follow what feels good it is the path of where I want to go.

I don't have to try to do anything or make anything happen.

I just follow what feels good.

Heather Hope Reed

July 3

E very day is a new opportunity to receive a million dollar idea.

Get yourself lined up to receive it.

Get in a good mood. Be happy. Do things you love doing even if it's just for a few minutes.

Make your intention to have a really good day.

The Inspired Entrepreneur

July 4

"We want you to get to the expectation of it coming easily." -Abraham Hicks

Heather Hope Reed

July 5

The happier you are the more you will realize from your vortex.

The Inspired Entrepreneur

July 6

Figure out how to have more joy in life instead of figuring out how to have more money.

The money comes from the joy.

Heather Hope Reed

July 7

F ocus on the vision of the business you are wanting to create.

July 8

There is no limit to what you can create.

Heather Hope Reed

July 9

Your thoughts are magnets.

The Inspired Entrepreneur

July 10

Everything was a thought before it could be manifested in physical form.

Heather Hope Reed

July 11

Your emotions fuel what you want to come faster.

Focus the majority of your attention on the things you love (or want more of).

The Inspired Entrepreneur

July 12

Keep any negative thoughts out of the conversation.

Stop yourself from talking negatively. Your life will imrove greatly.

Heather Hope Reed

July 13

Social media detox - remove yourself from groups that have a negative mindset.

Unfollow negative friends.

Pay attention to what you put your attention on.

The Inspired Entrepreneur

July 14

Turn off the news and unfollow any outlet that is negative or fearful.

Heather Hope Reed

July 15

K eep your thoughts about your economic future positive. Always positive!

The Inspired Entrepreneur

July 16

A llow your thoughts to go bigger.
Expand upon the vision you have.

Heather Hope Reed

July 17

I magine yourself having everything you want, how would you feel today from that place?

July 18

Check out YouTube videos about people who make a lot of money easily.

This helps to believe it is also possible for you and that it 's more common than you may think it is.

Heather Hope Reed

July 19

Happiness is a habit.

Make it a daily habit to focus on the things that you feel happy about.

Dwell in the happy thoughts.

The Inspired Entrepreneur

July 20

L et loose of the reality that you see.
Focus on the reality that you want to see.

Heather Hope Reed

July 21

B e more forward focused.
Focus on your vision of what is coming.

The Inspired Entrepreneur

July 22

Become addicted to your happiness.

Heather Hope Reed

July 23

Get clear about what you truly want.
Set the intention that it is yours.

The Inspired Entrepreneur

July 24

R elax more.
Take naps when you are tired.
Don't try to push yourself.

Heather Hope Reed

July 25

T ake a few seconds to visualize what you want. Do this a few times each day.

The Inspired Entrepreneur

July 26

F eel more at ease.
Relaxed, calm, at peace.

Heather Hope Reed

July 27

You live in an abundant Universe. Start by looking at the abundance all around you.

Go outside and notice the abundance of nature that sits in front of you.

Appreciate it and more will come to you.

The Inspired Entrepreneur

July 28

Your best strategy in your business is the one that is the most fun for you.

Heather Hope Reed

July 29

C are more about how you think about you than what you think others think about you.

July 30

F ocus on what you want, not what you want to get rid of.

Heather Hope Reed

July 31

C an you easily imagine yourself with a million dollars or more?

Keep visualizing your life with a million dollars until it's easy.

The Inspired Entrepreneur

August 1

Pay your bills with joy and peace. The better you feel about paying out money the easier it will be to allow more in.

Heather Hope Reed

August 2

B elieve more that all things are easily manifested.
Nothing is more difficult than anything else.

The Inspired Entrepreneur

August 3

D on't wish or hope. Expect!
Expect more to come to you!

Heather Hope Reed

August 4

You have to get out of the way more often. Stop trying to figure it out. Relax. Take a break.

The Inspired Entrepreneur

August 5

Meditate daily.
Relax your mind throughout the day.

Heather Hope Reed

August 6

L isten to your favorite music as much as you can. You will become more energized and inspired.

The Inspired Entrepreneur

August 7

F ollow your inspired thoughts today. (Everyday.) Whatever you have an urge to do - go do it. You never know where it leads you.

Heather Hope Reed

August 8

R eminder:
You can have anything you want, you just have
to decide and stay focused.

The Inspired Entrepreneur

August 9

Reminder:
Your thoughts about someone else will be felt by them in some way.

Keep good thoughts or don't think about them at all.

Heather Hope Reed

August 10

Everything is already lined up for you. All you have to do is line up with it. Be happy and expect it.

The Inspired Entrepreneur

August 11

"When money is not flowing, it may be time to start new activities that you have been wanting to do. Look for things you can do that will bring you Joy, aliveness, and energy, and start doing them. As you do, you will start your energy moving and create a flow of money." - Sanaya Roman

Heather Hope Reed

August 12

K eep focusing on the version of your business you are creating.

Focus on the aspects that are going well.

The Inspired Entrepreneur

August 13

T hink of yourself how you want others to perceive you.

Heather Hope Reed

August 14

Y ou must feel good and confident in your fee for others to pay you.

If you don't believe in your price, others won't either.

The Inspired Entrepreneur

August 15

I f you believe no one has the money to pay you, you will see that result.

Find examples of people easily paying.

Heather Hope Reed

August 16

T hink the best for others.

Congratulate their success and you will attract more of your own success.

The Inspired Entrepreneur

August 17

Always act from inspiration, not fear.
If you are fearful, get aligned first before acting.

Heather Hope Reed

August 18

H ave a positive outlook when pursuing something new.

You'll have much better results.

The Inspired Entrepreneur

August 19

You can do this.

You have the power of the universe inside of you.

Heather Hope Reed

August 20

Love more.
Love yourself.
Love others.

P.S. get a dog.

Love your dog.

The Inspired Entrepreneur

August 21

S et your intention for today:

I am focused on my joy.

Heather Hope Reed

August 22

Keep doing what gives you an immense pleasure.
In your life and business.

The Inspired Entrepreneur

August 23

C reate a vision for what you'd like to see happen and focus on that vision no matter what has physically manifested already.

Heather Hope Reed

August 24

Feel good, feel at ease, feel calm - with money and with your business.

Have more fun in your business.

Take more breaks.

Allow in more money.

The Inspired Entrepreneur

August 25

L et your goal be to feel unconditional happiness. The happier you are the more you allow in. You magnetize good things to you.

What are some happy things you can think about?

Heather Hope Reed

August 26

You have to keep lining up to what you want.

Line up the thoughts every day and watch how quickly you attract what you want.

The Inspired Entrepreneur

August 27

F ocus on the good as much as you can.

You'll attract more and more and more and more good things.

Heather Hope Reed

August 28

What is your IMAGINATION telling you? That is Source telling you what's coming. The Coming Attractions.

Follow that.

The Inspired Entrepreneur

August 29

"Nothing is inherently difficult. That's a belief system." -Bashar

Heather Hope Reed

August 30

Have as much fun getting to your destination as you think you will have when you get there.

The Inspired Entrepreneur

August 31

Practice the thoughts of the things you want until they become a dominate thought.

Heather Hope Reed

September 1

Your dream is always there.

The more you go back to it the more it becomes a reality.

It's always there just waiting for YOU to focus on it.

The Inspired Entrepreneur

September 2

It's so amazing to go with the flow each day following source and seeing where it takes me.

The days I tap into that flow are the best days. I am surprised and delighted around every corner.

Follow the thoughts and guidance that is always flowing.

If you let go of the negative thinking, the preconceived notions, the old belief patterns, you will be guided directly to what you want.

It's just a whole lot of fun.

Heather Hope Reed

September 3

I f you want it you can have it.

The Inspired Entrepreneur

September 4

You have to let go of the urgency.

Heather Hope Reed

September 5

You have to feel good and enjoy life in the moment.

The Inspired Entrepreneur

September 6

Y ou have to envision what you want in a fun and light way.

Heather Hope Reed

September 7

F ollow your impulses and really pay attention when you're onto something and when you feel REALLY excited about it.

The Inspired Entrepreneur

September 8

You always want to go for what you genuinely want and not what you think you can have.

Heather Hope Reed

September 9

M ake your intention for today:
"Today I will see the signs all around me."

The Inspired Entrepreneur

September 10

You are capable of achieving everything you want.

You just have to keep your mind on what you want and stay committed to a positive mindset.

Heather Hope Reed

September 11

You came here because you wanted to do great things!

The Inspired Entrepreneur

September 12

Be more of who you were born to be.

Heather Hope Reed

September 13

Where are you getting your business mindset from?

You have to pay attention to what you're listening to.

Is it your inner guidance or is it the "expert" who is telling you that it takes hard work?

The Inspired Entrepreneur

September 14

Make your intention today to become more magnetic to money.

Heather Hope Reed

September 15

W hat you accept as true will become your reality.

The Inspired Entrepreneur

September 16

As you open to love, you will experience a more beautiful world around you.

Heather Hope Reed

September 17

Y ou can have anything you want, but you must decide what it is you want.

Be a deliberate creator by deciding what you want and putting your attention on moving in that direction.

Don't decide what you want and then doubt yourself. That's going in the opposite direction.

The Inspired Entrepreneur

September 18

Align with your dream.

September 19

"The closer you are to alignment with what you want the calmer you feel." Abraham Hicks

The Inspired Entrepreneur

September 20

I have good news for you: What you want is on its way!

Heather Hope Reed

September 21

The condition (the problem let's say) you are focused upon is causing a vibrational response within you that creates your point of attraction.

Meaning whatever you are focused upon you will create more of because that is your point of attraction.

You have to stop trying to "fix problems" and focus on what it is you want.

So, the work is to catch yourself in the middle of fixing problems and moving your attention to what you want.

It can be a subtle distinction but you will feel it.

The Inspired Entrepreneur

September 22

T he success you're looking for is from within. The voice inside your mind that is guiding you. Your intuition. Your inner guidance. It's not from the outside. The people telling you what you need or should be doing. Follow your guidance and you will find your true success. The non-physical part of you is making the things you want happen. All you have to do is stop thinking in a negative way about what you want. It's "that simple."

Not so simple though, right. We've all been conditioned that things are hard to get.

So, the work is getting your mind back on track each day to what you want. That's the work.

September 23

R emind yourself this often: "I am powerful!"

The Inspired Entrepreneur

September 24

T hink thoughts that align with your dream (not opposing your dream) and allow the universe to line up the circumstances to physically manifest it for you!

Heather Hope Reed

September 25

T he universe is not testing you, it is simply responding to you.

The Inspired Entrepreneur

September 26

I f you want to have a better relationship with someone the best first step is to have better thoughts about them.

That's really all that matters.

Your thoughts are the most powerful things you have.

Heather Hope Reed

September 27

" It's not your work to 'make it happen'. It's your work to dream it and let it happen."
-Abraham Hicks

The Inspired Entrepreneur

September 28

T o get to your happy destination you have to be happy on the way.

You can't get to happy being unhappy.

Just focus on being happy today.

Heather Hope Reed

September 29

All your thoughts turn to something.

The Inspired Entrepreneur

September 30

You get to decide what you get to have.

Heather Hope Reed

October 1

Keep talking about the manifestations that have already come about.

Relive the feelings of it happening.

Milk it as much as you can.

It will help you to be inside your vortex more often.

The Inspired Entrepreneur

October 2

"Talk about what you want until you wobble, then stop right there.

Talk about what you want until you wobble, then stop right there.

Eventually, you'll carve out a path of a resistant-free vibration on what you want."

-Abraham Hicks

Heather Hope Reed

October 3

W rite the story of the life you want.
Write your new story.
Talk about it. Dream about it.
The more you do the more you will create the pathways of it happening.
It really is that easy.

(PS, you have to stop talking about what you don't want. When you talk about what you don't want AND what you do want you'll have a mixed vibration that won't allow you to move forward.)

The Inspired Entrepreneur

October 4

K eep following your inspirations.
They lead you to everything you want.

Heather Hope Reed

October 5

Honor how you feel about something. Don't try to cover it up to feel better.

How you feel about something is important.

It's guidance.

The Inspired Entrepreneur

October 6

Tell the story of how you want it to be not the story of how it always has been.

Heather Hope Reed

October 7

T ake control of the thoughts you think!

To be a deliberate creator you must think thoughts that give energy to what you want (not what you don't want).

Speak life into your life and business.

The Inspired Entrepreneur

October 8

T ake the action when you are really feeling inspired to do so.

If you're just trying to make things happen it will fall short of what you're wanting. Often nothing ever moves when you're trying to make it happen. Then, you get frustrated and say nothing ever works.

Get into alignment, get in a good mood, feel good, then follow the ideas that will flow.

Heather Hope Reed

October 9

I magine what you want more often.

The Inspired Entrepreneur

October 10

What do you REALLY want?

(Think about this question and write your answer.)

Heather Hope Reed

October 11

T he less "in a hurry" you are with wanting what you want the faster it will come to you.

Stop "trying to figure it out."

Stop "trying to make it happen."

Let go and be happy now. Be happy in the thought about the things you are going towards.

If you get out of the way, your manifestation will be fuller and more awesome than you could make happen on your own.

The Inspired Entrepreneur

October 12

The more pressure you put on yourself the more resistance you have.

You have to relax.

Give yourself a break.

Meditate.

Enjoy your day.

Have more fun.

Get happy.

Heather Hope Reed

October 13

F ocus on your level of happiness over anything else and you'll see how much better your life gets and you'll manifest what you want in record time.

Each morning, especially, take out your notebook and write about all the things you appreciate in your life.

You can use 4-5 subjects to write lists about to allow things to flow.

The more you appreciate the more you move the momentum in a positive direction.

The more you attract.

The Inspired Entrepreneur

October 14

T o get what you want you must believe that you can have it.

If you believe something is difficult to get, it's actually not true.

It's just your belief that it's difficult that is making it difficult.

Heather Hope Reed

October 15

My #1 Priority is to feel good.

When I feel good, my day goes really well.

When my day goes really well, I am happy.

When I feel happy, I build the momentum and feel excited about life.

When I feel excited about life, I see new paths to go down.

When I see new paths to go down, I feel good.
I repeat this daily as much as possible.

The Inspired Entrepreneur

October 16

Match the feeling.

It's the law of attraction.

The more you feel good, the more good will immediately show.

The more you feel abundant, the more abundance will immediately show.

The more love you feel, more love will come to you.

The million dollar ideas will pour in the more you feel like a million bucks.

Your job is to conjure the feelings of what you want for it to show up.

October 17

"Nevermind 'what is'. Imagine it the way you want it to be so that your vibration is a match to your desire." -Abraham Hicks

The Inspired Entrepreneur

October 18

"The secret of the universe really is to mind your own business. What we mean by that is: don't get so involved in the desires or beliefs of others, that you cause confusion or chatter in your own vibration and compromise your own alignment."

-Abraham Hicks

Heather Hope Reed

October 19

I f all you did was make your goal each morning to feel good, your life will come together perfectly. That's it.

Focus on feeling good.

The law of attraction will handle the rest.

The Inspired Entrepreneur

October 20

With strong desire and soft enough belief, you can create anything that has not been seen before.

Heather Hope Reed

October 21

Allow your cork to float.

Try taking time off from everything.

Let go of the feeling that you have to "be doing something" to manifest what you want.

Take the time off and let go and you'll start to float.

Once you're floating you will allow more in.

The Inspired Entrepreneur

October 22

D o what you feel called to do.

I see so many people checking in with everyone they can to help make a decision.

No! Don't do that.

Do what YOU want to do.

This is so vital.

Source is guiding YOU.

Heather Hope Reed

October 23

Y ou need to stop doubting.

Get strong with your thoughts.

When you wobble you lose your connection with the power of your energy.

The Inspired Entrepreneur

October 24

If you're strong and another is wobbling, you win.

You get what you want with your conviction of deciding that it's yours.

No manipulation needed.

You decide with your thoughts and energy.

Heather Hope Reed

October 25

Y ou attract what you are focused on.

Are you focused on castles or buttons?

The Inspired Entrepreneur

October 26

The "sureness" of your business comes from the sureness of your feeling about your business.

This was something that I learned while creating my business. I found when I "wobbled" my clients wobbled. Meaning if I had self-doubt or worry about them having issues or leaving, that's what would happen.

I had to become VERY emotionally strong regarding my business for it to flourish.

Heather Hope Reed

October 27

S tart believing it's easy.

Believe that the things you want, the business you want, is easy.

The Inspired Entrepreneur

October 28

You always have to remind yourself that it's attraction. It's only attraction.

You never have to actually "do anything" except focus on what you want.

There are so many marketing experts out there telling you how to manipulate others to buy from you, but they don't get it. You attract to you what you focus on. You decide your price and you believe in having it so much that you attract the clients who will pay it. Don't calibrate to the market. Calibrate to what you want.

This is life changing.
It's you doing what you want, living life on your terms, and being free.

October 29

Stop listening to others and listen to yourself. That's all.

Trust what you want is available and trust that you are capable.

The Inspired Entrepreneur

October 30

If you're going to make up stories about things, make up good ones.

Heather Hope Reed

October 31

You are connected to infinite intelligence.

You have all the answers inside you.

That means you are highly intelligent.

November 1

Your inner being is focused on the solution of what you're thinking about.

If you let go, you'll get the answer.

Heather Hope Reed

November 2

You have to do it the way YOU really want to do it. If you follow your own guidance you will succeed SO much faster than if you take the advice of others. Your guidance is telling you how to do the things to get to where YOU want to go.

Everyone is following each other and getting mediocre results (if that). Only follow it IF it excites you. There's absolutely no problem in getting expert advice in your business if you're excited and you resonate with the person. (Because you are being lined up with that person perfectly by The Universe!)

But, if you're doing it from a place of uncertainty, doubt, desperateness, don't do it. Only do it when it excites you.

November 3

If you're doubting something don't take action, yet.

Allow your guidance to take you there or some place else, or nowhere.

It's all good.

Heather Hope Reed

November 4

W atch the conversations you have with others.

The stories you tell are the stories you live.

It's really important to focus on the stories you want to live out. Don't tell people all the things you don't want or that have been going on unless you want them to continue.

Stay focused on moving forward to your new stories.

November 5

Believing that what you want is DONE, will make it happen.

Heather Hope Reed

November 6

F ollow where your interest takes you.

The more you follow the more your life changes.

The fun is in the creating!

Have a good time on the way to where you are going.

The Inspired Entrepreneur

November 7

An "I don't know" is a "No."

Remember, if it's not a "Hell yes, it's a no."

If you go ahead with declining, how do you feel?

Relieved and powerful or still in distress?

Follow how you feel.

Your energy is powerful and you carry it into each project.

Heather Hope Reed

November 8

If you think your service or offer is expensive then you will attract others who think so, too.

The Inspired Entrepreneur

November 9

Do a marketing strategy because it's fun and you enjoy doing it, not because you feel like you have to.

Otherwise, your energy won't allow it to work well.

Heather Hope Reed

November 10

S tay in the vision of what you want. Focus on the aspects of what you love.

The more you do the more you get closer and closer to what you want.

You're a magnet.

Close the gap between where you are to where you want to be by focusing on the vision of the life you want to create.

The Inspired Entrepreneur

November 11

"**A**nything that you give your attention to without contradiction, is going to be a very fast manifestation for you." -Abraham Hicks

Heather Hope Reed

November 12

You get what you worry about.

The Inspired Entrepreneur

November 13

Y ou can't force it, you have to allow it.

Think about all the things you cannot force.
You can't make things happen for the most part.
You have to allow it.

Heather Hope Reed

November 14

"**H**ow you feel is your indication of how much you're allowing yourself to be in the realizing state." Abraham Hicks

The Inspired Entrepreneur

November 15

If you focus on feeling good before anything else, you will naturally be on the right path to your desires. People ask me "how do I scale my business?"First and foremost, make feeling good your highest priority. Each time I find myself feeling kinda "ugh" I instantly remind myself to think a different thought, one that will make me feel good.

"I'll ask myself, what can I do right now to feel good?" or "what can I do to have fun in this moment?"

When I do that, I change my vibration to what I do want and then the inspiration flows.

Your inner guidance knows how to get you to where you want to be (scaling your business, or the love of your life, or more money) it's your job to line up with that by feeling good.

November 16

When you're in the Vortex there is no effort.

Focus on feeling good, then do what is inspiring to you.

The Inspired Entrepreneur

November 17

Affirm:
I easily get paid in my business. Money just flows in.

Heather Hope Reed

November 18

Talk less, receive more.

The Inspired Entrepreneur

November 19

The better you feel means there's more momentum toward what you are wanting.

Keep focusing on feeling good.

Heather Hope Reed

November 20

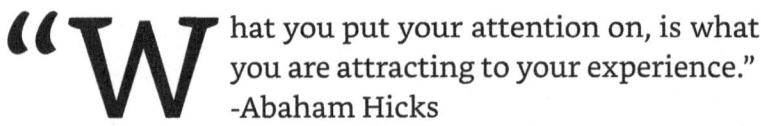

"What you put your attention on, is what you are attracting to your experience."
-Abaham Hicks

The Inspired Entrepreneur

November 21

Move in the direction of who you are.

Heather Hope Reed

November 22

Decide on what you want and keep your focus on it.

Focus on having it and experiencing it. Feel good about it.

The Universe/your inner being will guide you to it with ease.

The Inspired Entrepreneur

November 23

Focus on the business you want and not on how hard it's been.

Soon you will have it.

Heather Hope Reed

November 24

W hen you stop being impatient the ideas will flow.

Take pleasure from your ideas and not rush them.

Feeling impatient will not get you anywhere but frustrated.

The Inspired Entrepreneur

November 25

B y the time you have the thought/vision of something it already has a lot of momentum.

You don't have a thought, an idea, and then have to create it. It's already created vibrationally.

All you have to do is align with the idea.

Go with the flow.

Allow.

Heather Hope Reed

November 26

The goal is to be a vibrational match to what is in your vortex.

It's already done.

Your work is to get yourself in the vibration of having it and it will be yours quickly.

November 27

Believing that what you want is DONE, will make it happen.

Heather Hope Reed

November 28

The manifestation of what you're focused upon the most will happen.

Keep your focus on what you want most.

Keep your thoughts there.

The Inspired Entrepreneur

November 29

I f it's not active in your vibration, law of attraction will not bring it to you.

Being active in your vibration means that you have focused upon it, talked about it, told the story of it, thought about it.

You can stop focusing upon something unwanted and it will go away.

You attract based on your focus.

That's why I say your focus is your SUPERPOWER.

The more you focus on something the more it is coming to you. Use your focus for alllllll the things that you want.

November 30

Y ou are creating your life with your thoughts in every moment.

Keep focused on what you want, not what you don't.

Everytime you focus on what you don't want you are creating more of that.

Keep focused on where you want to be.

Know you will get what you want the more to focus there.

The Inspired Entrepreneur

December 1

B elieve in your dream and your dream will manifest.

Heather Hope Reed

December 2

Receive an idea, hold that idea in your mind without resistance and watch it become.

You are so powerful that you are able to create anything that comes to your mind.

Anything.

The Inspired Entrepreneur

December 3

What you appreciate, appreciates.

Heather Hope Reed

December 4

"When you believe something is hard, the universe will demonstrate the difficulty.

When you believe something to be easy, the universe demonstrates the ease." -Abraham Hicks

The Inspired Entrepreneur

December 5

Y ou are creating your reality by the thoughts and words you use everyday.

Change your reality quickly by changing these in the direction you want to go.

Heather Hope Reed

December 6

R epeat after me:

"Something special is going to happen to me today!"

The Inspired Entrepreneur

December 7

Always focus on what you want, not how it will happen or the cost of it, or how much you will make from it.

When you focus on what it is you TRULY want, everything comes together so perfectly!

Heather Hope Reed

December 8

P oint your focus in the direction of where you are wanting to go. The more you do, the faster you will attract it.

The Inspired Entrepreneur

December 9

What traits or characteristics do YOU believe someone with a million dollars possess?

List those out on a piece of paper.

Now, start feeling that way in your life.

Heather Hope Reed

December 10

Don't look for the solution, look for the alignment, it will bring the solution.

The Inspired Entrepreneur

December 11

"If you want it to be, it's meant to be."
-Abraham Hicks

Heather Hope Reed

December 12

If your desires don't feel good to you then you're not lined up with them.

The Inspired Entrepreneur

December 13

Your work is to believe what you want.

Heather Hope Reed

December 14

I magine everything you're working on is going along perfectly.

The Inspired Entrepreneur

December 15

Always be focusing on what you want to happen instead of what you don't want to happen.

Heather Hope Reed

December 16

F ocus on one thing that brings you happiness and the rest will follow.

The Inspired Entrepreneur

December 17

"It is as easy to create a castle as a button. It's as easy to manifest something that feels really big as it is to attract something that feels really easy. But, you have to make the thing that feels really big, feel really small." -Abraham Hicks

Heather Hope Reed

December 18

"**B**ig thinkers better get lined up with source energy."
-Abraham Hicks

The Inspired Entrepreneur

December 19

J ust chill.

Heather Hope Reed

December 20

When you can't get something to work, you will have to let it go.

That might mean you need to take a break. Go do something else.

You may even need to quit it completely and see what happens.

When you're able to let go of that resistance your cork will float.

The Inspired Entrepreneur

December 21

Keep thinking, keep visualizing, keep daydreaming, keep looking at what it is you want.

It will naturally come to you.

Heather Hope Reed

December 22

To change your life you must change the way you look at yourself.

Create the identity of who it is you are and start seeing yourself as that person.
You have to stop saying the negative things about yourself.

"I'm not good at (fill in the blank)." STOP SAYING THAT.

Focus on the things you are good at and the things you are now becoming good at.
Your words (beliefs) about yourself are vital.

You gotta change the way you look at yourself.

December 23

My statement for today is: The valve of unlimited wealth is opening.

Heather Hope Reed

December 24

Once you feel at peace and feeling good, you will be able to follow the thoughts that come into your mind.

Those thoughts are from source.
Listen to them.
Notice them.
Pay attention to them.
Take the inspired action.
Bam! Manifestation.

The Inspired Entrepreneur

December 25

To really make a change to your life you must see yourself as the person you want to be.

Create that new identity and daydream about it every morning.

Doing that little bit will build the momentum and you will start acting in ways that line up with that new identity.

It's automatic.

Heather Hope Reed

December 26

Your impatience of it not being here yet is holding you where you are.

Pay attention to the journey. It sounds so cliche', I know, but the joy IS in the journey.

So relax and focus on the fun you can experience today.

When you relax you allow your cork to float and that's when you allow all the good stuff in.

The Inspired Entrepreneur

December 27

Write down how you want things to go today. I do this nearly everyday and it manifests.

The Inspired Entrepreneur

December 28

You can have anything you want. You just have to keep focused on what you want, without doubt.

The Inspired Entrepreneur

December 29

Y ou gotta stop looking at reality.

You're creating more of the same. (Unless your reality is how you want it to be.)

Heather Hope Reed

December 30

"We want you to train yourself into unrealistic thoughts. We want you to stop all of this realism you have going on. We want you to stop facing reality and start creating reality. Because it will change in the moment that your vibration changes." -Abraham Hicks

The Inspired Entrepreneur

December 31

"If you're able to imagine it, it's not unrealistic."
-Abraham Hicks

Heather Hope Reed

About The Author

Heather Hope Reed

Heather Hope is a Manifestation Coach, Writer, Teacher, Speaker, Podcaster, and YouTuber. She has an audience from over 100 countries. She speaks on topics of business, money, love, emotions, and alignment.

Made in the USA
Monee, IL
24 April 2023

32338115R00236